In the Jitterfritz of Neon

by

Damien B Donnelly

&

Eilín de Paor

First published 2021 by The Hedgehog Poetry Press,

5 Coppack House, Churchill Avenue, Clevedon. BS21 6QW

www.hedgehogpress.co.uk

Copyright © Damien B Donnelly & Eilín de Paor 2021

The right of Damien B Donnelly & Eilín de Paor to be identified as the authors of this work has been asserted in accordance with the Copyright, Designs and Patents Act 1988. All rights reserved. No part of this publication may be reproduced, stored in or introduced into a retrieval system, or transmitted in any form, or by any means (electronic, mechanical, photocopying, recording or otherwise) without prior written permissions of the publisher. Any person who does any unauthorised act in relation to this publication may be liable for criminal prosecution and civil claims for damages.

ISBN: 978-1-913499-32-7

Cover photograph © Damien B Donnelly, taken at the Cité de l'Architecture et du Patrimoine musée, Paris.

The Cottonwood Café was first published in The Broken Spine Artist Collective: Fourth Edition

Contents

Introduction 4
Opening Moves 9
The Cottonwood Café 10
Two Hens in a Basket 11
The Irregularity of all that is New 12
Trying to Identify a Taste True to Ourselves 13
First and Last 14
In Amsterdam We All Rode Old Bikes 15
Habitat 16
A Glitterball is not a Wrecking Ball 17
I Miss You 18
Diamonds are not for all Girls 19
146 Essex, Lower East Side 20
Learning to Not Name Everything 21
When we could 22
Promises Made at Lombards 24
Last Call 25
Edging 26
Dear Old Best Dress 27
Things We Can No Longer Fit Into 28
All In 29

INTRODUCTION

"I first met Eilín by a dolmen in the Phoenix Park, in Dublin, at a live Spoken Word event in 2018, the first live performance for the pair of us, and following that we twice had dinner together, once while I was on holiday back in Ireland and the second time, having just returned to live in Dublin, at an Indian restaurant where you brought your own wine and where we regaled each other with tales of nights out already distanced and giggled at the expectations of all the soirees still to come.

Little did we know, back then, at that tiny metal table in a covered courtyard that all those expectations would be put on hold less than one month later with the arrival of Covid instead of courses and continued conversation.

Over the following year, there have been times when nights out from years ago have felt closer than the possibility of future plans which seemed like dizzy dreams which is why it has been such a pleasure to twist the sounds and tastes of my past nights under the glitterball with Eilín's while counting down to the opportunity to make new ones together."

Dami x

"Life, if you're lucky, is long and memories stack up like books on a nightstand. There are the meaningful ones, the love and loss ones, the serious and important ones, but the memories I go back to again and again are the wild ones. Nights out that started without a plan and ended-up an adventure, hours' long conversations that evolved into debates, theses, setting the world to rights, encounters with strangers that led to unexpected friendships, even the sad nights that felt like endings.

I've missed making new wild memories this past year. I look forward to making more when we can all meet again. A night out with the wondrous Damien B. Donnelly is top of my wish list for when that time comes. I hope you enjoy this little trip down the cobbled lanes of our night out memories and that it sparks memories of your own."

Eilín x

"Most glorious night!
Thou wert not sent for slumber!"

from *Childe Harold, Canto III*
Lord Byron

OPENING MOVES

Mixed fruit, after chess, in an open café,
in August, heat still on high after sunset.
I was to be married to Amy, for a season,
recently met though forever to be friends,
for you can say that when you're young;
can promise forever and discard it, later
like bitter bishops and one knight stands.

Mixed fruit, after chess, in the Open café,
in Paris; apples, oranges and occasionally
cherry tomatoes who just couldn't sit still
and kiwis who hadn't settled in their skins,
all of us upended in a basement restaurant
with cutlery and crayons, drawing designs
on napkins because we'd only discovered
the words for how to doodle and to dream.

Amy was Queen, cherry of the Big Apple
proffering to pawn her orange-shirted Joe
even if Vincent's regard of blue steel was
like no fruit I had ever taken to my tongue.
Mixed fruit, after chess, considering ways
of sectioning slices, wondering if a Kiwi
should really be eaten with all its skin on-
there were apparently bears in our bunch.

Mixed fruit, after chess, coming together
to tempt a complement toward a cocktail,
not knowing that nobody knew each other,
not caring, just daring the other to expose
a little more of the flesh we were all dying
to taste. Mixed fruit as Queen takes Rook.

DBD

THE COTTONWOOD CAFÉ

I know the place existed.
I can still see the rockabilly maîtresse d' snaking
between gingham tables in her matching head scarf,

a platter of wings and celery balanced on each palm,
puffing aside a bleached ringlet as she
flicked the record set-down lever with a hip.

I see your dark eyes in candlelight,
your smile, perhaps, wicker-clad chianti,
cigarettes, of course.

We were spick and gleam, groom-sheened,
joints like clean-greased bearing wheels.
When the bill came, we kept our fingers hooked.

It was where the alley door of *Bewley's* was.
No one else seems to remember,
but I know it was there.

E de P

TWO HENS IN A BASKET

for Lisa

Once you've careened by shopping trolley
down a cobbled street in Glasgow,
pakoras seeping warm oil through the paper in your lap,
there really isn't any other way to travel.

The moon was a grapefruit low over Sauchiehall,
casting body-shaped shadows through keyholes
of the locked spare bedrooms
of the Gartnavel nurses' residence.

Back when no one needed us,
when being quiet was for thinking up the next plan,
when ground floor windows were a curfew dodge
and a midnight dip in a hospital pond passed for romance.

We decked our rooms in pound shop boas,
picked up dresses in bargain bins,
kept just enough each week for two for one
chimichangas and cheap early entrance to *Clatty Pats*.

I spent my last fiver of the summer
smuggling *Ben and Jerry's* in my carry on.
You lent me the bus fare to the airport.
We never did make it to *The Burrell Collection*.

E de P

THE IRREGULARITY OF ALL THAT IS NEW

for Sonya

You haven't lived until you see how the other half live-
until you've fallen out of a gay bar of 5 floors at 5:00am
and climbed onto the back of your cousin's bike to careen
across the canals of consciousness you never considered

where eels sliver like snakes, like the strange straight men
who sniffed you out in that gay bar, although you're a girl
and confused as to why a letch had climbed up to camp out,
finding out how the other half move; dancing on tabletops-

shaking your Beyonce bits with topless boys and bottoms
bashing their guavas against grooves in a bar, on a street
not a single foreigner ever comes close to pronouncing-
the Reguliersdwartsstraat, in early morning Amsterdam,

that regular cross street where you ran your fingers along
the freedom of irregular tastes, the drunkenness of dawn
not yet crossed over into unconsciousness, the night before
you both lost at being stoned. You, on the back of a bike

on the way to the Pijp and the stairs that leant like ladders
to the stars, your nose touching the steps on front of you
as you ingulfed all that was new. You haven't lived until
you can say you've seen how the other half simply live.

We never did make it to The Dillon, that following night.

DBD

TRYING TO IDENTIFY A TASTE TRUE TO OURSELVES

The 1ˢᵗ drink I bought myself at a bar
was a Malibu and pineapple. I'd taken the mother's tongs
to my long hair to eradicate the curls; the frizz that alluded
to the parts of me not yet finished.

That meant all of me.

I wanted to be slick, like them, like she was
with the island air diluting in the glass I had to copy,
like he was with his side flick and his ease with everyone,
always on other sides of rooms

I was forever trying to cross.

Even the river divided Dublin in those days
when pineapples only accompanied ham on sticks
for the Nouvelle Cuisine and no one could identify
a coconut still in its shell.

It tasted like unseasonal smellies mothers opened
under tinselled trees mixed with potpourri and that exotic
yoghurt I tasted at Santa Eulalia, at 5, when they served
spaghetti paler than Irish skin with not a trace of tomato.

The first mistake is trying to be something else.

DBD

FIRST AND LAST

The beautician enters, calmly instructs –
I am to drop the robe and follow spatter-laminated signs.
Five counts per pose, if I want an even job.
She leaves me to strip.
The timer beeps.

ARMS UP. LEGS SPREAD.
I notice the still open window blind.

ARMS OUT. FORWARD STRIDE.
A tabby glares from a nearby ledge.

ARMS IN. SWITCH LEGS.
A young man stalls as he leaves his house.

TURN AROUND. BEND DOWN.
The brakes of a double decker bus.

A ten minute airing before
I am dry enough to dress
and leave my backlit frame.
I gag at the whiff of chemical skin.
The cat smirks: she knows I missed a bit.

E de P

IN AMSTERDAM WE ALL RODE OLD BIKES

Soft curve of well-worn wheel around canal-

we were always on route to somewhere else;
a Sloe gin on the corner of the Leidsegracht,
Jack and his coke along that terrific terrace
of Icebreakers where the cyclists cut through
the orders and throw away jokers of heated
card games while our tempers and summers

melted in glasses like ice, like shirts;

opening themselves up to fine fragrances
of fresh flesh as other boats moved off

to search for more desiring docks.

We inhaled everything then; those glasses
we never imagined running dry, cigarettes
getting wet on edges of ashtrays & attitudes
while 20,000 bicycles all peddled past us,
on route to another place, to touch, to taste,
to tie up, for a time, to open and to inhale

the soft scent of things that we'd well worn.

DBD

HABITAT

We own this land of high-end gins, stalking the botanical savannah
with a clink of ice queen heels –

not the girl with tatty lashes in her glitter balm skin,
not the man spawning sweat to a throbbing disco beat.

Aglide on crumpled wings, set to a crosshatch symphony
of weathered hands and crinkled brows,

we sashay through the parting crowd
anointing all who turn to bow.

E de P

A GLITTERBALL IS NOT A WRECKING BALL

We wanted to own that dancefloor on the 1st floor
but the glitterball never cast enough concern
onto the pulse of poppers everyone sniffed,
under collars, as if no one wanted to be caught,

as if no one knew all you could divine from a scent,

as if no one really wanted to identify the truth
of all we ground down on the 1st floor; at the Block,
on the corner of George's Street & one-night stand,
on the compromise of community and being caught out,

as queer.

We danced our way through the 90s, owning nothing-

incognitos in ice queen heels as we inhaled the fumes
in the face of all we were being told we could not have.
Sometimes I saw lads lick the floor; chase white lines

looking for anything pure under all that was shadow.

In the 90s, in Dublin, on that 1st floor of a hot Block
redolent of poppers & sweat and the cigarette stains
of life and its limitations, there was barely a glitterball
big enough to knock the blocks we needed to wreck.

DBD

I MISS YOU

in the tumble of neglected streets,
the jitterfritz of neon,
the silent rain of cobbles,

in the shuttered shops,
the echo of the busker's strum,
the wind-skipping cans and paper cups,

in the necessary meals,
the 90-minute bills, the empty tables
in spaced out rooms.

E de P

DIAMONDS ARE NOT FOR ALL GIRLS

I wonder if we went back to that bar where every inch of skin
was tattooed like the truth was too good to be seen

would we find a part of ourselves still considering cocktails
and how long we could continue to mix all that was not meant

to be a match.

We smoked then, consoling the weight in between the liquids;
the black diamonds, to sit outside in the silent rain of cobbles

and shiver in skins that didn't feel right, blowing smoke rings
that disappeared like our thoughts, like our hold, like that ice,
wishing we could lasso them around each other,

to make us stay, to make us say; *yes, I love you, je t'aime,
moi aussi,* to make them swallow us whole and spit us out;

reborn, reshaped, having found a finer flesh, this time round.
Sometimes, we ordered cocktails we didn't like the taste of
and we'd smile

and ask questions to the boys with their tats who'd take them
back, replace them with something better suited to our tastes.

Sometimes, I think we too were cocktails waiting to be served
in correct glasses and to be held in the right hands or maybe
we were just like the ice;

melting in between the heat of a mix never meant to match.
Sometimes, I wonder if the parts of us still there are the parts

we never wanted to keep, like all those cocktails we sent back,
now waiting, by defined tats, for somebody else to order them.

DBD

146 ESSEX, LOWER EAST SIDE

The Secret Guide to New York brings us to a restaurant fronted
by a pawn shop – a glamourous take on hardware pubs
back home, where you can pick up bailing twine and drill bits
for your Sunday DIY, while your pint of Guinness settles.

Waiting for our number to come up on the host's impassive clipboard,
I catch a glint beneath the counter – emeralds in black velveteen –
a costume paste link necklace as vivid as any gem, as expensive too.

I covet it, all through cocktails and overpriced linguine, crave it's weight around my neck,
like the snake a petshop keeper draped across my shoulders once on Capel St.,
tongue flicking, geometric head – the yoke and ballast of her.

Leaving for our cab, I ask to see it, note a turn of irritation in the sales assistant's lip.
How many times has he shown this chain to women with holiday eyes
after one too many Proseccos? It's not emerald afterall, I see,
more a fescue blue: mildewed at the links, uneasy in its viscose nest.

E de P

LEARNING TO NOT NAME EVERYTHING

It started in Dublin;
drunken confusions in The Front Lounge
with chandeliers we thought sparked us better

but artificial light has no correlation to the truth.

The others came in
from behind, not really strange in our community
but I wasn't used to back doors, then or delusions

of names while they slipped into The Back lounge.

We were lost for an hour,
in the one bar with two entrances and two different
names. In the early days, it's all about naming things

later, identity is less demanding and more innate.

Much later, in Cork,
sitting on bare barrels in that dizzying bar that held
no chandelier, they whispered about the other place

long before No Name had become The New Name.

I decided camouflage
was how we'd camp it up in Cork. But after leaving
the barrels and all their women behind for a left bend

down a dark street, we eventually came face to face

with the place of their whispers
sign posted, literally; The Other Place. Sometimes
things are named with intention to delude but then,
at other times, they're so direct they easily deceive.

DBD

WHEN WE COULD

meet mid-morning, foggy from the night before, sunglasses, sinking
   into butter leather chairs,
be brought mimosas and French toast, cascading with berries and syrup,
   jazz, low, Bessie Smith singing
Need a Little Sugar in My Bowl and we'd have it: be dripping with it.
   A taxi to the coast
for a walk in dunes. Salt sea breeze would make us think again of cocktails,
   so we'd get lost for an hour,
trying to find the right break in the sedge to reach the road, shake sand
   from our toes, unroll cuffs,
tease our hair into something presentable, find a bar with outside tables
   serving vodka with frosted rims
to top back up our sugar levels, trade summer stories, think it would be good
   to see beauty before the sun sets,
so we'd bus back into town, visit *Chester Beatty,* where the wine-draped
   exhibits would remind us of cheese
and how long it'd been since the syrup, so we'd find an enoteca, feast
   on burrata, ciabatta, Nero d'Avola.
Friends would join, through impromptu texts and window passings.
   We'd get too big for the table,

sharing plates picked clean, extra bottles emptied by "One more glass please,
   for my friend", move the party,
take a left bend down a dark street, arrive to *Fleetwood Mac* as the night
   takes over. We'd find a banquette, pile
bags and jackets precariously, take turns minding them, buying rounds, have
   conspiratorial catch-ups in toilet queues
and smoking areas, but mainly dance – for what seemed like days – dance
   until one by one, we'd slip away
through soft-washed streets, on a promise to do it all again another night.

E de P

PROMISES MADE AT LOMBARDS

That haunting, that dance;

we brushed soft shoe against hard surface,
the pre-millennium stream of slow smoke;
jazz notes under low lights down at Lombards
with its wine by the bottle so that we swayed
to those notes too complicated to catch hold of.

We were saxophones, playing pink elephants
between the duke's darkness and the white lights
of the blinding dawn. Prisoners to the poison,
we stepped across that floor, already haunted,
devouring desire before it was kissed by the ghost

we'd promised each other not to shake.

DBD

LAST CALL

The ammonia waft of laneways tangs exotic in my throat.
I let the pub door swing shut, stop to watch
the swans of *Water's Edge* arrange their necks for sleep,

judge the thinness of shoe soles, the thickness of June air,
the quicksand of memory and the distance
of cobbles between me and bed.

Taxis will come when I click – bumble warmly
across the bridge. I sip the glitter of the stippled lake,
drain the summer's swollen dregs.

E de P

EDGING

Sometimes, tease tastes better than the truth,
sometimes touch is a print left on the same glass
centred on the table that divides your thoughts

from my tongue,

your flesh from my fuck. Sometimes, just to tease
the thickness of the June air, I reached for that glass
at the same time, just to touch your hand, to look away
and laugh as if it were a mistake when my finger tasted
the hair on the back of your hand like I'd just drank
from the liquid running down along your spine;

the sweet sweat, running onwards

to that sweeter spot I knew I'd never saver.
Sometimes I'll order a white wine just to consider
my options, knowing my lips have a fondness for red
but velvet can distract, comfort too can be confusing,
but white wine; you don't fold yourself into something
crisp, but there are times when all you want to feel

is its crunch within your clutch.

DBD

DEAR OLD BEST DRESS

In a green that flatters
and with hip pockets, your seams
accommodating months of little movement
and extra helpings, trusty companion
so many nights before, so few of late,
you glide on with a drape –
thread fern memories, furled with promise.
Soon you'll reach your limit, defeated, join
the relics of the forsworn half of the wardrobe.
I'll scour the online rails for a replacement, settle
for something navy, with no place for my fists.

E de P

THINGS WE CAN NO LONGER FIT INTO

In a box,
suffocating beneath the black of the wardrobe,
somewhere in between distracted & defeated,
a stash of beermats is wilting.

A collection
of since crushed cardboard connections
I once curated; silly souvenirs of drowned youth
when the world was a poll & flexibility
no limit to position.

In that box,
scented of stale ashtrays & the golden gorse-tinged
taste of Malibu, are boozy beermats from various bars,
stained with various orders we quickly knocked back
before growing tired of their taste,
drying

next to calling cards
that no longer connect, that are no longer
so susceptible to suggestion.

There are pieces
of crushed cardboard slowly suffocating
under all that black, in the forsworn half of the wardrobe
where you cannot actually see the collected remnants
of all that no longer fits.

DBD

ALL IN

September shambles in –
a washed up bagged out dancer
in laddered tights
eyeliner smudged
the smell of last night's fags
clinging to her straggly locks.

Breakfasting on stale baguette
and lukewarm Lilt she
elbows to the game table
hoicks up her skirt
claims a stool
stakes her chips and
with a jaded flop
lays the busted flush of summer
on the pill-worn baize.

She takes her own time
tongues a last breadcrumb
from between her teeth
gathers up her things
smooths down her skirt
heads back to work.

E de P

www.ingramcontent.com/pod-product-compliance
Lightning Source LLC
Chambersburg PA
CBHW021455080526
44588CB00009B/859